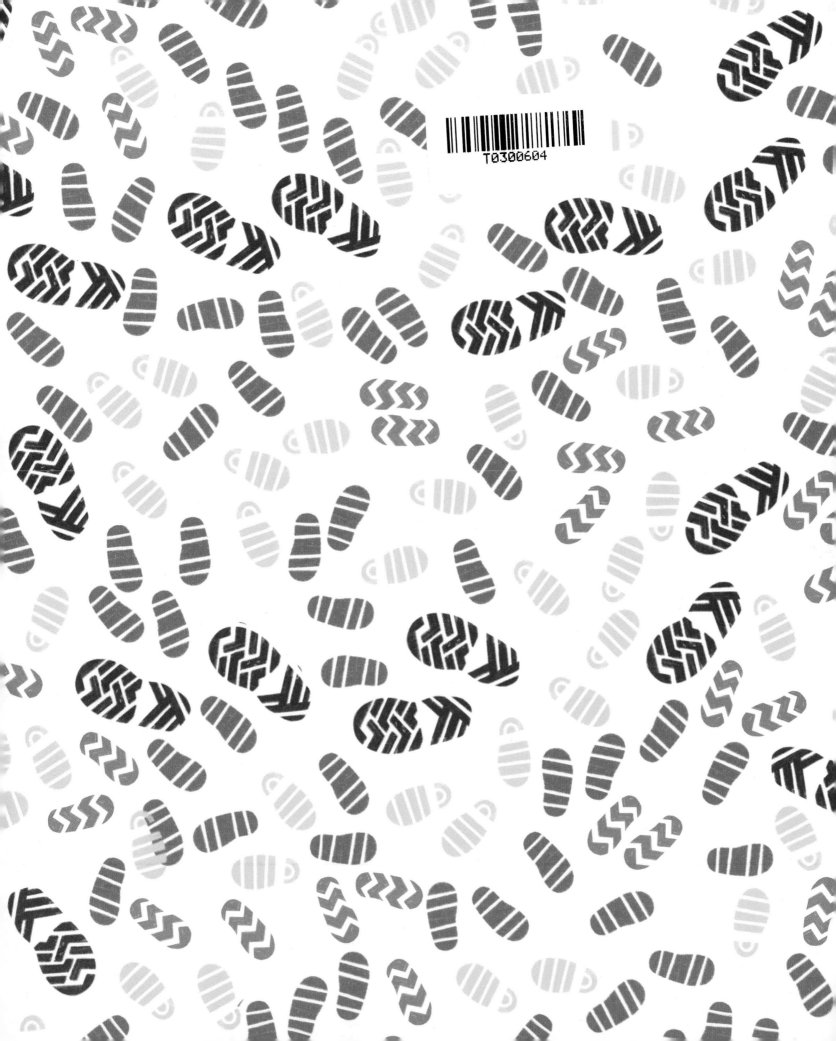

Ranger Hamza's
ECO Quest

Illustrated by Kate Kronreif

IVY KIDS

Hello, I'm Ranger Hamza.

You know, nature is full of incredible
things—from the tiniest seed, to the
biggest whale, to all of us. We all play our
part in looking after our wonderful planet.

In this book, we'll go on an eco quest to discover some of nature's wonders, and we'll find out the important roles they play in our environment.

Let's go!

Pitter-patter, the RAIN falls down,
plants can suck it from the ground.
The rain barrel collects the rain
for thirsty plants to drink again.

Rainwater is precious.
Plants need water to grow
strong and healthy.

A rain barrel is a container
that collects rainwater.

We can reuse the rainwater to
water the plants in hot, dry
weather when there is no rain.

Let's make a mini rain barrel!

Find an old bucket or container. Make sure it doesn't have any holes!

Put it somewhere unsheltered where it can collect rainwater.

Use your rain barrel to fill a watering can and water thirsty plants in your house or garden.

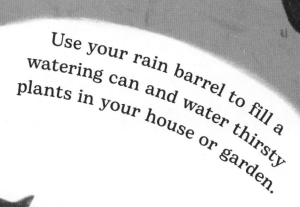

Lots of happy flowers, fruit, and vegetables!

Bushy. Crusty. Leafy. Dusty.
Squidgy. Dotty. Flaky. Spotty.
Blue, green, white, or gray.
Can you spot LICHEN on
your walk today?

Lichen comes in lots of
different shapes, colors,
and textures.

You can spot lichen
on rocks, walls, twigs,
and tree bark.

It offers food and
shelter to many very
tiny creatures.

Lichen loves
to grow in
clean air.
Lots of lichen
growing in an
area can mean
the air is low
in pollution.

There are three main types of lichen:

flat lichen

shrubby lichen

leafy lichen

How much lichen can you spot growing where you live?

Leave a patch of grass unmown
and let the DANDELIONS grow.
Please don't think of them as weeds,
as they can feed the hungry bees.

Dandelions have green toothy
leaves and bright yellow flowers.

They are a great
source of food for
hungry insects early
in the year.

Dandelion seeds are like
little parachutes that
float away on the wind.
The seeds can land and
grow in unusual places.

Be a weed champion!

If you have a garden, leave a patch of grass to grow so dandelions can thrive.

See how many dandelions you can find where you live. They can even grow in a crack in the sidewalk.

Can you spot any bees, butterflies, or ladybugs visiting dandelions for a sweet treat of nectar?

Up in a tree,
sat on a branch,
a nest of BIRDS' eggs
waiting to hatch.

Most birds lay their eggs in a nest.
They build them in many different places.

Some birds choose dense hedges
to keep their precious eggs safe.

Other birds build nests in
buildings, or even hide them
in the grass on the ground.

You can help birds save energy by putting out nesting materials for them to use.

Place twigs, grass, moss, and lichen in a bush or hanging basket for birds to collect.

Some birds make their nests using mud. Help them by making a muddy puddle on the ground.

A bridge across a road, or a river flowing.
A hole in a fence, or a grass verge growing.
What do all these things share?
A WILDLIFE CORRIDOR is found there!

A wildlife corridor connects
two habitats together.

They provide a safe route for
creatures to move between
areas in search of food.

These corridors can be
BIG like hedges or a
row of trees . . .

. . . or they can be
small, like a strip
of long grass.

Look for a
wildlife corridor.

Go to a garden or park and imagine you are a tiny creature, like a mouse.

Is there a safe route you could take to get from one side of the park to the other without being seen by a predator?

A DEAD WOOD pile—let's peep inside!
A safe, cosy place for insects to hide.

Dead wood is wood that is no longer living. You can find lots of different types, like fallen trees, tree stumps, or sticks and branches that have fallen to the forest floor.

Dead wood may not be living, but it's still very important in nature, providing shelter to lots of minibeasts.

Make a dead wood stumpery for beetles.

If you have a garden, dig some holes in the soil and "plant" upright logs in them.

On a balcony or terrace, you can plant logs in a tub.

These log stumps will attract beetles to lay their eggs.

The SNAIL slithers, silent and slow,
leaving a silvery track.
The snail is never far from home,
as their house is on their back!

People often think of snails as slimy
pests, but snails are an important
food source for other creatures.

Snails are like nature's
clean-up crew. They eat
rotting plant waste.

Go on a snail hunt!

Look for snails hiding in shady spots, under leaves or on the side of plant pots.

A snail can change the shape of its body to fit inside its shell safely when it senses danger. Very gently lift a snail by the shell to see this disappearing trick.

ACORNS grow on mighty oaks,
each in its little cup.
But look, here comes the squirrel,
who loves to eat them up!

Acorns are a type of nut that
is the fruit of the oak tree.

They are an
important food
source for wildlife.

Squirrels collect and bury acorns, so that they
have food to eat during the colder winter months.
Sometimes they forget where they've buried them,
and these acorns can grow into new oak trees.

Try growing a new oak tree from an acorn.

In fall, find a healthy acorn with no insect holes in it.

Fill a small pot that has drainage holes with compost. Put the acorn into the compost, so it is about an inch from the surface.

Water the pot and place it outside. Wait to see if an oak tree sprouts in spring.

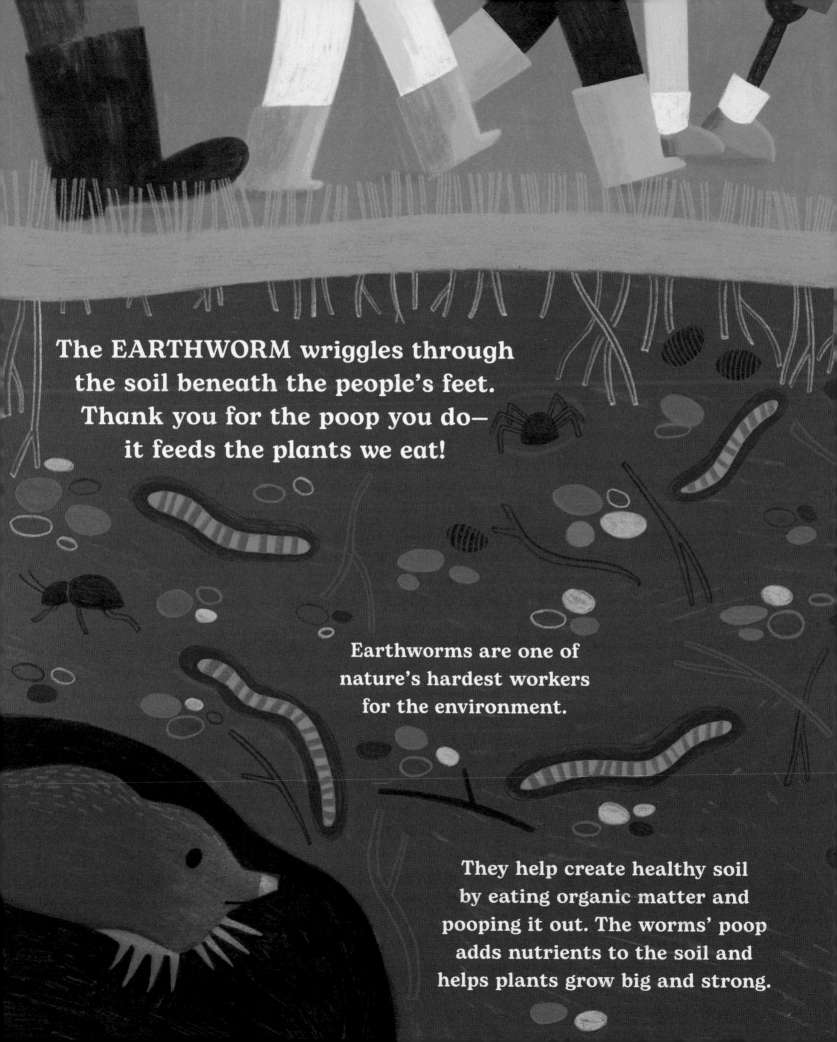

The EARTHWORM wriggles through
the soil beneath the people's feet.
Thank you for the poop you do—
it feeds the plants we eat!

Earthworms are one of
nature's hardest workers
for the environment.

They help create healthy soil
by eating organic matter and
pooping it out. The worms' poop
adds nutrients to the soil and
helps plants grow big and strong.

Make a mini wormery to see worms in action.

Fill a large glass jar three-quarters full with alternating layers of damp (not wet) soil and sand. Put a handful of dead leaves and vegetable peelings on the top.

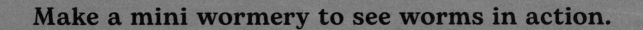

Add some garden worms. Wrap the jar in black paper so the worms are kept in the dark.

Keep the jar somewhere cool, like a cupboard, for one week. Then remove the paper to see how the worms have mixed up the soil and eaten the leaves.

The SUNFLOWER stretches up so tall,
it peeps above the garden wall.
Its face turns slowly to find the rays,
of the blazing sun on summer days.

Flowering plants like sunflowers
are real eco heroes.

Flying insects love their pollen and nectar.
Then, in fall, the flower heads dry out and
their seeds become an important food
source for birds during winter.

Grow natural bird feeders—sunflowers!

Grow sunflowers
in your garden or
on a balcony following the
instructions on the seed packet.

When the
flower heads start to
droop, cut them off. Store
them somewhere warm and dry
for a couple of weeks until they
completely dry out.

Poke a hole all the way
through each of the dried flower
heads with a sharp pencil. Use the holes
to string the sunflower heads up outside
where the birds can feed from them.

See the SEAWEED on the shore,
all washed up in a line.
Slippery, slimy, slick, and shiny,
and smelling of salty brine.

Seaweed grows in the
ocean, rivers, and lakes.

It comes in all different
shapes, sizes, and colors and
provides a food source for
many ocean creatures.

Over half the
oxygen we
breathe is
created in the
ocean, much of
which is made
by seaweed.

Spot different types of seaweed.

There are many different seaweeds, but they come in three main types, called red, green, and brown seaweed.

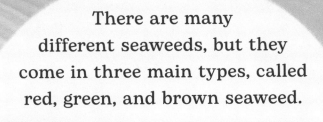

Next time you visit the beach, see if you can spot some seaweed that has washed up onto shore. What color is it?

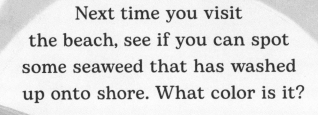

The TREE'S tall branches brush the sky,
their leaves are lush and green.
These friendly giants cheer us up,
and help keep our air clean.

Trees are the biggest
plants on the planet.

They release oxygen, which we need
to breathe, and provide food and
shelter to hundreds of animals,
birds, and insects.

Some tree species are particularly
resistant to air pollution and can help
filter harmful pollutants by trapping
them on their leaves and bark.

Make a guide to the trees in your neighborhood.

Walk around your neighborhood and take photos of the trees you spot. Take close-up pictures of the leaves and bark and other features.

Use tree guides or the internet to identify the trees you have found.

Make your own local tree guide by drawing pictures or printing the photographs of your neighborhood trees. Write specific descriptions of your particular trees.

bark

There's an animal you will see everywhere,
it looks just like me and like you.
Look in the mirror, you'll spot one right there—
that's right, HUMANS are animals too.

Human beings are a part of nature too!

Just like the other eco heroes in this book, we can play our part in helping the other living things on the planet stay happy and healthy.

Although humans have damaged the environment, we can use our big, clever brains to solve the problems we have created.

Here's how humans are helping the rest of nature:

Creating wildlife corridors through cities for insects and wildlife to safely travel along, by planting wildflowers on road verges and on city roofs and building little tunnels so animals can cross busy roads.

Bringing animals back to areas where they have gone extinct, to help the other creatures in the ecosystem who depend on them. This is called rewilding.

Here are some more ways YOU can be an eco hero:

Walk or cycle instead of traveling in the car whenever you can.

Visit different wildlife habitats and learn how you can help to protect them.

Make sure all the trash your family makes, like cans, paper, and plastic or glass containers, is properly recycled.

Find a nature project or group near you that you can join.

Care for your belongings so they last longer. Repair them instead of replacing them.

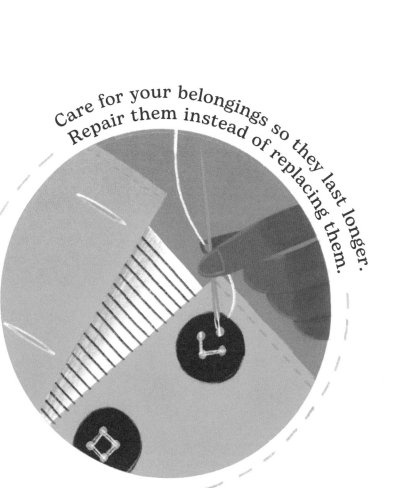

Talk to your friends and family about the things you learn about nature and how we can all help it.

And remember, wherever you are you can go on an eco quest. Just keep your eyes open for these wonders of nature when you are out and about. Nature is everywhere you look!

For Ava — K.K.

At Ivy Kids, we know that our readers will inherit the world we create, and we owe it to them to be constantly improving the sustainability of our publishing process.

The paper this book is printed on is certified by the Forest Stewardship Council as made from 100% post-consumer waste, meaning no new trees have been felled to make it, and less water is used compared to virgin paper production. This book can be recycled.

By buying a copy of this book, you have made a choice to support a more eco-friendly way of publishing. Thank you.

Text © 2024 Hello Halo Productions Limited. Illustrations © 2024 Kate Kronreif.
Text developed with Terri Langan.

First published in 2024 by Ivy Kids, an imprint of The Quarto Group.
100 Cummings Center, Suite 265D, Beverly, MA 01915, USA.
T +1 978-282-9590 F +1 078-283-2742 www.Quarto.com

The right of Kate Kronreif to be identified as the illustrator of this work has been asserted by her in accordance with the Copyright, Designs and Patents Act, 1988 (United Kingdom).

A CIP record for this book is available from the Library of Congress.

ISBN 978-0-7112-9174-4
eISBN 978-0-7112-9176-8

The illustrations were created digitally
Set in Bogart
Published and edited by Georgia Buckthorn
Designed by Sasha Moxon
Production by Dawn Cameron

Manufactured in Villatuerta Spain, on recycled FSC paper, GC032024

9 8 7 6 5 4 3 2 1